Spring Rains

Scott MacKeen

BookLeaf
Publishing

India | USA | UK

Presentation by *BookLeaf Publishing*

Web: www.bookleafpub.com

E-mail: info@bookleafpub.com

ISBN: 9789360947989

First edition 2024

For Mom and Sara

A Different Face

A different face forgets me
Where time stopped and the truth fades
I feel the shadow of the pale-blown hands
Run through me, suddenly
Looking another way
I see your face over the burning coals
Louder, more beautiful
Between the night and the dawn

Memory

The sound of it comes cracking off the water
beyond the caves, like October smoke

threading back the dead folds of summer
I become still in my glowing

flickering about these great rooms blindly
reaching, like some faint outline in glass before
dawn

the mountains shake the little sea out the
window
the unclear face I see outlined is me

stretching this cold, mad star to the wall
folded in—the vacancy of millions of years
passing me by

each day, I run through the trees, calling vibrant
odd things from out of the wind, tumbling like
empty paper

half in moonlight; where memory through the
rain comes
drifting along the buzzing shore by the rocks

waiting to be lifted and rearranged, in the acres
of waves
with the few trees, facing back to winter

The Far Edge of the Pond

Day pains have been nodding me out. Terrifying
time.
I watch from afar, the birch wood crackling dead
in the water.
On the tracks underground, still pounding old in
earth,
a cool smoke dissolves through a dream of light
by the dry road. In the still air, the moon skates
up to dark.
A clear snow begins its long life, at the far edge
of the pond.

Spring Rains

5

From a highway below the rocks, holding in a
line   they are falling off again
content in a sea moving well-made   they
slip through   in a cloudless way, low likes
minds well-guarded   appearing less
youthful in the dark fire I make myself turn to
the cold, damp roots   below   its banks of
snow rising again   becoming a river ready
to run down   there: the dead-end highway
sitting at the other end   burning the sun up,
straight as ever my heart is familiar with the
dust   finding its way to the night
it carries on a flutter of wings that fold inward
bending alone with endless optics
confronting space through the wood rim
on foot the leaf shades fighting speed

***

going past the sleeping ground I walk   I hear
the shadow breathe, becoming hope again
            woven to rise by light, collected and put
away   under the dead folds   the body beside
me here is young   infinite of an image lost
to us in the wild   burning gold all year

into nothing   the emblem sounds like the
weight of a slow wind   correcting time with
reason   we could not see, between storms
        the stillness in this power, at the window
the fear in motion whispering down
proclaiming a soul, or the substance of the light
itself   on a vision path   hearing the
black walls flood up over the fountain
renaming horizons before the rain   I draw
around you   what it was   I kept forgetting
to be

Cracking Under

The trapped ice packs are out there on the lake
gleaming in the moonlight, three layers down.
The wintering heart weeps through the waters,
fishing in the eyes of the outer dark.

Here in a last stand against night
squared up south, it runs heedless,
clamping its familiar limbs to me like a ghost—
leaving a flying that glows, as suddenly as a
child

breaking from the enduring frost. Outwitting
time.
The mounted-moon-place it dreams,
where the sun and stars all space down, before
the new grass.
Nothing imprisoners me up here, hoisted out—

love comes and goes suddenly. Flushed long
from the dark, under the rubble along the shore.
I catch you, running back across the paddled
cliffs
in shadow, balancing fear with your light

Suspended deep. It reappears like the power of
the sea
in freedom, waking slow upon heaven. The
world passes,
unearthly still. Towns around us whisper in the
growing pool,
as the whole motion comes flying back over
me—

The heavy lines gliding like ribbons, mounting
the sky
in a steady run. Still seeing the flames you ran
down
from the sidewalk, cornering me in a way:
Where did they go?

I know the words I can't say, running inward—
each time I've dreamt of being home again,
climbing the long-dead sea upended like magic
we descend first. Caught up in eternity, like fire
runs

along each track in the ice, the sun heals,
as the thin air turns us to a new end
with the loud miles of the country it weathers:
in one, long voice.

Evening in the Mountains

The voice of my spirit stopped
And you were quick to answer
In return—
The hollowing escaped from the waves
Like a great fire, cut clean to dry land.
Seeing the faceless trees put out the old pain
again
I sat with a star, puzzling it over.
All the shouting down the rugged mountain
All evening
Beginning to leap up now,
Through the un-marveled nerves of the night.

Wildflower Blooming

I picked a wild rose and the singing rose was
free
In the cycle I can make myself dark as the world
As the hearts are made to order
Always now
Always yearning, brought nearer in our hands
Like this wildflower blooming
Out under the sun
Reliving a common endurance
Broken long ago

Antigua

The garden was set against the wind
And the turquoise sea
The red roses flowed out over the arches
Like a crimson mound all around us
This picture
Between our two feet, changing itself inside
In our new land for awhile
Twenty layers up, we got here
Going against island after island
And making it to the next without question
I saw it for myself
A bay in the shadows, and warm below
A brief summer with no fear
I know what it can give you
And ask for no more upon returning
The other revealed within
His awing eyes, laboring as they go

***

Back
Bringing myself back
To the wall
The light under a tree
Two twins gulls out over the heart in the dark

On a beach in April
Fragmenting the moon from a glance
Like a ship in glass your eyes awake
The landscape we pass through
As the heat runs through, to the breathing end
I tell you on another day
Our sacrifices in hope belonged to no one here
No place, but turned on a dark wire
Deep down a patient sea
Turning unborn, after hours

***

I was searching
On another native island sleeping more
When I listened, traveling with the blind
lightning
Dying out among the echoes
I knew most of the faces
They say, there is family in the empty places
Not knowing where this or that
Place can turn
Moments in a life, by instance
When we had left the garden
Suddenly knocking in the mud
Like strangers, the sight of ourselves
Could not have found us settled
I wake again
And time reverses to a glow

Like midnight on the tide
Lit low
 We had flown away amid the roar
And returned home to the ringing spirits

Cherry Leaf

I gaze upon this cherry leaf, commuting its
shape
in a great flash of light. Yielding wind of no
assurance.
I know it pulls away with nothing to stop it.
An abundance of things clever and grim
keeping it unaware—a fact of happy life
Never entirely its own.

In Dreams

The nameless in the stars from where I sit
Like a shell start to break off, somewhere in the
dark.

Fixed like a hawk, the branches sway in ritual
Beyond the door where the lights come on

Through the windows, in parallel shadow.
Falling by our own ways, we walk the air, so
sweet and cold,

As brilliant as the sea before us: memory
Where we find ourselves following a voice like
we'd dreamed

The mastery of distance and time, on the way
down
There is complexity to the deception, you say

The mind itself is a poor impression of nature
A broken specter of reality, drawn together

Till pride and pressure take the air out of one last
thought
And I know perfectly well its lonely impulse

To enlarge me like a flame, down a long harbor
of voices
Calling from out the night, or hovering up there
from above.

I Climb

My chest swells as I go up and up
From the center
Not even a fool's light blazing
Amid this hill
Two autumn boots set forth
To conquer direction
Speechless, steadfast as ever
I climb
With the suffering spearmen
Soft-footed on earth
A ghost gleam spins before me
Lessening the past in flight
And once more I rise the high wall
In view of you, leveling off
These poor mistakes to shame
In reckoning over the city
I climb
How long I've waited
For what you speak of
Flocked; I am knowing
The fool in me
Crossing the sky with a level heart
And these spirits are with me
Cold like smoke
Held high up

Constantly saddled to space
In cells, too, moving things
Between life and death
Surging love to the solid spot
I know, after the winter's ice
I first began to step—
So fast
The magic made known to me
In a dream I entered
Weeping, with the souls of angels
Glazing in the frost fields

***

Who will understand this absence
Weightless of letting go?
At the end of something
We began
Holding for them all
In one
A certain heart, steadying behind me
Thinking, on the edge of the water
I want to stand with you on this earth—
I want to tell you I love you
Simply
For what it's worth

The Swan

The death-defying swan wanders like a queen,
counting itself in tragic beauty
in the stirring rain. Through its lips,
the wind quickens through to me—
lingering in the misty night, breathing low.
How this broke at last! Who knows how!
The earth air glorifies me in the new summer
something wild and old, darting back through
the trim grass
out over the country. Rivers, moons, colors,
rising—
growing hours, clearer in shape. We pass the
magic thread,
giving the night a loose, dim glow, lifting the
lake in purple.
By all means which track the far sky
shaken to its own grove between winds.

Beneath the Dim Lake

The person you thought you drove out from
drives under, with all the old voices
under the moon.
Of course it's an old trick childhood plays
showing us how it moves on
or sometimes sticks out like stone
from beneath the dim surface
hollowed out to one wave, alone—
as in memory.

From Dreams to Birth

Dreams: That break like water, as I move along the shadow of water.

Love: Sped through the garden in a sudden quartz of sun upon a white door.

Knowledge: Took to being, unmoved, on the knife edge of nothing.

Memory: In the teeth of the cave, pressing my hand because it is a part of me.

Death: Deeply clumsy, white pond without answers, dipping down to drink.

Birth: So I may always remember what you came to be.

The Sleeping Country

Diagrams of lost wind are being measured up
here tonight.
Great rivers: thinning out in a heap.
In an hour, I will fall half from life
to sleep, becoming some crowned, impassioned
thing,
marbling out alone across the hills.
Voices depart—on the fray of a hymn,
startled to light. Farther down the road,
moonbeams away, in a glow of power
not at all my own, it speaks down in the dwell of
time
on the pavement. The river snows in a sky of
fire,
streaming in moon-buckets of leaves, down to
earth.
I shake a north cure from out of the granite—
the ghosts labor themselves for the fall.
The crumbling smoke stalks out for change.
Whirlwinds in return clangor paleness out of the
snow.
In the same way, framed in a window
lurking feeble through such devotion,
my parent's thin roof is being unbridged again.
With a flee—

The moon through which I walk is heaven-bare.
I lie cool down and break, in a certain way,
drawn clearer down through the halls of white.
My solemn stowing. I've lost all to make this
right.
The island rounds out, out here; I see now
My father's old look in me. There's no terror
steeping up.
Eyes I can see pretend to sleep.
The machinery turns too tight.
In a pace of circles, forgetting I'm alive, I come
slow to your side.
Odd powers through rooms, wind gradually into
place.
In the high middle step, shining,
near the water, the horizon folds out
nearly unstoppable.

Summer

The sun—a soft face—starts to ripple the tide,
starts to shake enormous to get out.
Each word, a song lifts out of the weeds.
I sink down through, like a long-bewildered
sleeper
coming into a force, half-mounted.
That thing my soul spoke of—under the snow—
can clear all the souls of us, or leave us frenzied
to piece the long clouds after midnight.
I step through the gate. I don't recall finding the
middle air
molding this sand.

What's that, which brushes my right eye?
Which dance with the lips of frozen birds,
faded in flight? By a small window of darkness
ducked in calm beauty along the low field,
my roots run to a place of flowers.
Through the flocks I enter
A star on the hill rises in one place above the
city;
a tree bends. The quick stones charge
underwater.
Love stands like a bridge across time, in so
many cities

thirsting with their obsessed oceans, for the dark.
Sending in rain over the crooked arcs of brick
and marble—
going over, to fall. I dream of you, fixing my
eyes
to hold my body where I lie, no more cold.
Like the receding wave I thin out of night.
Out of the desolate substance I broke in two.
I saw the wilderness in you,
as though everything like summer grows in
white,
beyond the thumbing tide.
Passing a hundred steps before I go on.
Before love never was.

At Dusk

While the world moors in certain ways to a halt
As though recalling grief tucked away in mind
By the cornerstone with no past
Knowing nothing comes real before fear
For long we walk overhead with the helpless
ringing
You held for me
Even so, I can hear the shadows of a skyline
Of cities sifting over
Mulling, how it came to me
In its solitary way
Morning after morning there were the faces
Of another time, at the foot of our bed
Rephrasing the question with a word again
A new beginning
Thinking of losing you after all, myself
The ways the little soul shines to grow up
The part of forgetting
It is the old echoing of a country
Sinking its poles in with the bones of nature
Each tip breaking the axis to dark
And I think I'd die from this beginning
Starting too badly in my rung position
Starved to be gutting away in soft pieces
Of my design

This is the attic of my hours up here
This time
My last cup of wine
And I'll see these empty streets again
Knowing where you are, I'll howl
And move that way
Like a crooked vulture of faith

December

The wild white in glitter tilts up, to cut the sun at
mid-space.
Out from the edge of the limb I climb
and it comes to close a little more each time—I
climb out.
Each night, it reaches my unknown page.
Or like the domestic weight of April, desperately
moves on.
It may even be the disappearing power of the
light
somewhere far off, where it flows out in the
same silent flash—
turned to dark. I stay outside the boundless drop
of the moon.
Across the harbor, I see the heaped-out mud
roads widen to pieces
both ways. The heat dozes south, in its silent
ways of desire.
Like the water I rise. The sound of it rushing
through my blood.
Time falters like the restless shadows in sand,
the tide will change it.
So to think itself over. In its place: like the new
composite we move in.

Reflecting in itself the inner sweetness of a life,
between two worlds.
I stand with the quiet smoke of the valley,
digging down.

One More Flower

I'm picking one more flower   studying the
sky above   the felled tree   running over
and over   rolling the world as far as I lie
I know it moves its moral weight to me   burning
in hand like a shower of hope   kissed to life
as wild as the wood I touch   the front of a
new dew   melts to spring I begin to see it
once more   bellowing out all day
bounding unspoken labor beneath me   I close
the door   inside the great cloud
renewing the thunder around my heart

John

Wise gluttons sing the earth, hitting their thumbs
to music.
Back an inch, the atmosphere. In swift passion.
I know of space. It becomes mine, through the
clear stretches
a million miles down. Clean, on the pocket-light
element.
Between sorrows, signs of turns beginning.
Furious beauty.
Welcome to spring, old John. I have spared
plenty to find you.
You were right about the sky. It hovers insisting,
one eye to the road
of blackness that beckons us. Not the other way.
You juggled the whole mountains of snow,
dripping in the dark.
Titled a little to one side, as if I didn't know.
What made you want to drive your car a
thousand miles,
with your fundamental engine. Fighting.
Insisting.
Without force or forethought. Minutes turn to
hours.
My brain gets too stimulated at night. You keep
telling me.

This is your righteous honor: wandering past the
stirring sounds of night
 on your drowsy wire, about the height of a man.

Angel on the Fishing Wall

33

Angel on the fishing wall
You know the shape of things when they fall
The dark stands longer the closer I walk
So cry to my ears then put an end to talk